How to

How to Write About
POETRY

A Pocket Guide

Brendan Cooper

PETER LANG

Oxford • Bern • Berlin • Bruxelles • New York • Wien

Bibliographic information published by Die Deutsche Nationalbibliothek.
Die Deutsche Nationalbibliothek lists this publication in the Deutsche
Nationalbibliografie; detailed bibliographic data is available on the Internet at
http://dnb.d-nb.de.

A catalogue record for this book is available from the British Library.

Library of Congress Cataloging-in-Publication Data
Names: Cooper, Brendan, 1980- author.
Title: How to write about poetry : a pocket guide / Brendan Cooper.
Description: Oxford ; New York : Peter Lang, [2019] | Includes bibliographical
references and index.
Identifiers: LCCN 2018050911 | ISBN 9781788747288 (alk. paper)
Subjects: LCSH: Poetics. | Poetry--Study and teaching.
Classification: LCC PN1042 .C587 2019 | DDC 808.1--dc23 LC record available at
https://lccn.loc.gov/2018050911

Cover design by Brian Melville.

ISBN 978-1-78874-728-8 (print) • ISBN 978-1-78874-729-5 (ePDF)
ISBN 978-1-78874-730-1 (ePub) • ISBN 978-1-78874-731-8 (mobi)

© Peter Lang AG 2019

Published by Peter Lang Ltd, International Academic Publishers,
52 St Giles, Oxford, OX1 3LU, United Kingdom
oxford@peterlang.com, www.peterlang.com

Brendan Cooper has asserted his right under the Copyright, Designs and Patents
Act, 1988, to be identified as Author of this Work.

This publication has been peer reviewed.

Contents

Acknowledgements

Many thanks to Faber & Faber for granting me permission to publish "The Forge" by Seamus Heaney in its entirety.

All fires of poetry need to be lit. I would like deeply to thank three inspirational teachers, Julie Bufton, Lindsay Gibbon, and Nick Gleeson, for lighting mine over twenty years ago.

This book is dedicated to my parents, my wife Nouska, and my two daughters, Manon and Hermione: the most precious of poems.

Introduction

If you ask secondary school or university students what they find hardest about studying English, you won't always get the same answer. Inevitably, individual students will harbour their own individual, personalised concerns – bits of a course they find tough, maybe; or an author they have grown to hate; or a particular text through which they have been grimly struggling. But the most common answer is fascinating, since it is the form of writing at the very heart of English literature – the lifeblood of a supposedly unrivalled literary heritage running through immortal names like Chaucer, Shakespeare, Milton, Wordsworth, Keats, and beyond. When students are asked what they find hardest about English, the most common answer, by far, is poetry.

Many students will say that they simply *don't get* poetry. They are confused by it, and struggle to understand it. Poetry seems, too often, not to make sense; or, even worse, to make only partial sense, masking a clear message behind irritatingly obscure or vague language. In that oft-used response, "I *don't get* poetry", there's also a different kind of accusation. Many students don't really get why poets bother writing poetry at all. What's the point of it? Why produce these weird little things called poems? What's the story, when it too often seems as if there isn't much of a story to tell? Of all the things students have to deal with and to master in the subject of English, poetry most often presents the biggest challenge.

As well as suffering from this reputation for difficulty, poetry is also often accused of something even worse – of being *boring*. A classic "introduction to poetry" lesson – and one that I've used many a time – provides a good example of this point. The teacher writes the word "POETRY" on the board, and immediately goes round the room, asking pupils to call out the word that first comes to mind in response. The teacher then writes their suggested words on the board – surrounding the word "POETRY" with pupils' single-word replies. It's an interesting exercise; the board becomes a kind of scattergun mind map of the whole room's perceptions of poetry. Almost inevitably – and certainly every time I've tried it – there will be someone in the room who, perhaps along with a wry smile, or a snigger, or a look of amused contempt, offers up the word "BORING". There it is, the awful truth that the teacher doesn't want to accept: poetry is *boring*. Once again, the question about the actual point of poetry looms its ugly head. What is it for? Why *should* anyone care about it? It's fair to say that, in many quarters – especially amongst young people – poetry suffers from something of an image problem.

The idea that poetry is of little interest or relevance in the contemporary world is certainly not a new one. But we live in an ever more screen-based world, of ever increasing speed – a world that feels, to many, like it is increasingly unsuited to the slow-paced contemplation of poetry. In the technologically glittering environment of twenty-first-century culture, the argument that poetry is superfluous feels like it is gaining greater and greater force. In a 2013 *Independent* article, Nathan Thompson bleakly declared that "poetry is dying". Stories have abounded for years about the struggles of poetry publishing, the lack of a market, the difficulty in making poetry sell. The often rather fragile sales figures for poetry could easily be seen as clear evidence of its limited influence. As Jay Parini has frankly summarised, "Poetry doesn't matter to most people. That is, most people don't write it, don't read it, and don't have any idea why anybody would spend valuable time doing such a thing". And yet, there are signs, too, of a contemporary hunger for poetry – of new avenues opening up via technology and social media that might allow poetry to be accessed and enjoyed in fresh ways to a younger, more varied audience. According to a 2018 article in *The Bookseller*, "poetry book sales have seen a 66% increase in the past five years". It should be added, though, that much of this apparently thriving market depends on a very small number of "superstar" successes (like Rupi Kaur, whose *Milk and Honey* sold over 1 million copies), while the vast majority of poets struggle onwards, neglected and unread.

In the context of education, this becomes a serious and important challenge. Why, after all, *should* students engage with a form of writing that can feel so divorced from reality? Why bother to grapple with writing that seems, so often, deliberately written to confuse, and to obscure straightforward meanings? Put simply, for thousands upon thousands of students across the country – even ones who might passionately enjoy other forms of literature, like novels and plays – poetry can feel like an alien phenomenon: an outdated genre, imposed on them by equally outdated academics and teachers.

This is a guide for any student who has ever felt uncomfortable with – or distant from – poetry. It is designed to be concise, to the point, and clear. Its purpose is simple: to provide some "ways in" to the reading of poetry, as well as some ideas and guidelines about how essays on poetry might best be approached. If you have ever felt at sea, when asked to think about and to write about poetry, this guide should provide you with some welcome assistance.

It is my contention that there is a connection between the false belief that poetry is boring, and the false belief that it is difficult. There is a danger, in trying to say "oh, poetry isn't actually *difficult*", of sounding patronising – like an academic snob, showing off some intellectual superiority. But the point is not so much about how clever anyone is – it's about *how* we read, and *how* we think about poetry. When approached in the right way, poetry is often much less difficult and much less confusing than it first appears. Too often, the structures imposed on students by our education system – *especially* in relation to public examinations – can reduce poetry to a dry series of technical components. But this is the last thing poetry really is. It can come as a real surprise to realise that poetry is not, in fact, written for the classroom. In stark contrast, it is almost always written by poets who have never had any intention of being *studied* at all, many of whom, in fact, would say that the last thing they want is for their poetry to be subject to academic scrutiny in a classroom environment.

At the heart of this guide is the belief that poetry is often sadly misunderstood. The pressures surrounding our education system and exams can distort poetry into a simultaneously complicated and tedious technical exercise – an infuriating crossword puzzle to which there must, somewhere, be "answers" that require finding and decoding. But this gets poetry all wrong. Poetry is not some old-fashioned expression of dead experience. It is not some elitist demonstration of intellectual superiority. It is not some dry, fusty fulfilment of formal technicalities. It is a distillation, in words, of ourselves: a word-mirror that we can hold up to ourselves, in order more fully to understand who we really are. As such, poetry is a serious business. Any practical guide to writing about poetry needs to be based around this key point – that poetry is a much deeper and more passionate phenomenon than the mechanical approaches of classroom study suggest it to be.

So, what are the best ways of reading and understanding poetry? How should tricky matters like "form" and "structure" best be handled? And are there some good, clear, practical strategies that might come in useful when writing about poetry? Let us begin.

CHAPTER I

Why Is Poetry Difficult?

The Confusion of Poetry

It is a familiar situation. A piece of paper is placed in front of you, with a poem printed on it. You are asked to read it, in preparation to write an essay. There might be some bullet points underneath, asking you to focus on things like "language", "form", and "structure" – or maybe more specific things like the poet's use of rhyme, or rhythm, or stanza structure, or "poetic techniques", whatever they might be. You skim the poem. Bits of it make sense. You think you can see what it's about, broadly speaking. But some phrases, some lines look odd, confusing. You can see that it rhymes – but you can't for the life of you work out what to *say* about the rhyme or how it works. It's written in stanzas – but so what? Aren't most poems? What are you supposed to make of that? Despite having a few ideas, you don't feel confident – you can't escape a feeling that there are deeper meanings at work that you can't see. You are sure that there must be an "answer" to this poem, but it's somewhere beyond your reach, and all you can do is sit there staring at it in frustrated confusion.

Why do poems feel difficult? The answer, I think, has something to do with the experience I describe above. Too often, it can feel like we need to deal with poetry in this sort of purely mechanical, technical way – as if its purpose is to be a puzzle, there to be deciphered. As if a poem – like a mathematical equation, or a scientific problem, or a quiz question – has a definitive "answer". It is not really the fault of teachers that this idea is so widespread: after all, in order to satisfy particular examination criteria, teachers have to explain the relevant assessment objectives and to present a clear framework of approach so that these can all be satisfied. But poems do not really have "answers" in any straightforward sense. It is when we try to look for simple answers in poems that things begin to feel tangled and confusing, because we are, effectively, looking for things that aren't really there. We become like medieval crusaders, desperately searching for a Holy Grail that we will never be able to find, for the simple reason that it doesn't really exist. In such a direction madness lies.

This is not to say that poetry is easy, or that there is some simple secret trick that, once discovered, makes writing about poems a piece of cake. It is a question of understanding *why* poems are written in the first place – a pretty important question, when you think about it, but one that often gets neglected in the context of academic study. Because poems are not written in order to deliver answers. In contrast, they tend to be written in order to explore and to expose problems, conflicts, or contradictions in our experience – to express the complicated reality of what it means to be alive in the world. Poetry, in other words, is fundamentally *opposed* to the mechanical frameworks of examination assessment we are so often caught inside.

So if poems don't have *answers*, how, exactly, are we supposed to read them? What are we supposed to look for? The key to unlocking the door of poetry can be encapsulated in a single word: ambiguity. What I want to demonstrate is that poetry, above all – more than any other form of literature – deals in ambiguities. A good poem will never just mean one thing – it will mean many things, all at the same time. Far from finding a single "answer" to any poem, the sensitive reader should actively look for these ambiguities, and use them as the heart of any written response. A student who can become comfortable with this key point about ambiguity will have the art of writing excellent essays on poetry at their fingertips.

Case Study in Ambiguity #1: "The Sick Rose"

As an example, I want to take a well-known poem by William Blake, a poet who often appears on examination set text lists at the secondary and university levels. Blake is a perfect poet to look at with regard to ambiguity, because the poems for which he is most famous – the *Songs of Innocence and of Experience* – seem, at first glance, to be almost childishly simple, but become more slippery

and complicated the closer we look. He is the perfect
example of a writer whose poems seem easy enough on
the surface, but are in fact tricky to analyse (the trickiness
becomes greater once we realise that he also engraved
images alongside his poems, which often comment on the
poems in curious and unexpected ways – but we won't go
into that here). Here is a short poem by Blake, entitled
"The Sick Rose":

> O Rose thou art sick.
> The invisible worm,
> That flies in the night
> In the howling storm:
>
> Has found out thy bed
> Of crimson joy:
> And his dark secret love
> Does thy life destroy.

What is going on here? How should we interpret these brief
lines? On first reading, the poem seems simple enough. It
is, literally, about a rose: a traditional symbol of the beauty
of nature. The poem is a kind of lament for the damage
inflicted on the rose by a "worm" – another feature of the
natural world, but one with rather less pleasant and positive
associations. The rose here is "sick" in the sense that it has
been harmed – its petals eaten away, we presume, by the
worm. In this reading, the poem is a fairly straightforward
nature poem. It reflects on both the beauty of nature, and
also its fragility. The ruthlessness, even the brutality of the

natural world is emphasised, with the rose's death at the worm's hands an emblem of the inevitable cycles of life and death surrounding all living things.

So: simple enough. A nature poem. A flower poem. A "sick" rose, eaten up by a nasty wriggly worm. Does this fairly literal interpretation, though, make sense of all the details Blake uses in this poem? A close examination of the poem's language reveals a few curiosities – a few strange moments that look like they require consideration. Why, for instance, is the worm "invisible"? It's an odd adjective to use in order to describe a worm. It *can*, of course, be interpreted as consistent with the literal reading we have already identified. The worm is "invisible" simply because it's dark – as the following line clarifies, the worm "flies in the night". In other words, the worm is not actually invisible – it just cannot be seen. But the word also reso-nates with associations of the supernatural that cannot be completely ignored. Blake's language, "the *invisible* worm", suggests that this might be something more than just your everyday worm. "Invisible" suggests something spectral, something ghostly (supported, perhaps, by the fact that this worm somehow "flies" through the air). It leads us, in other words, away from the literal interpretation of the poem we quickly developed, towards something more *figu-rative* or *metaphorical*.

On top of this intriguing detail, other curiosities gather. Why, in the seventh line of the poem, is the worm described as male? For a creature like a worm, we might expect it to be described with the generic "its", rather than

the masculine "his". In addition, how could a mere worm
harbour something as sinister as a "dark secret love"?
Worms don't love; humans do that. Here, Blake is giving
specifically human qualities to something that is non-
human (there is a technical term for this, which is *anthro-
pomorphism*). What are we to make of these details? In the
light of them, the poem starts to feel less like a straightforward nature poem, and more like a much more human
tale. The worm becomes a threatening figure of masculine
power, imposing itself – himself – on the feminine rose,
with disastrous consequences. His love is not only hidden
and "secret", but also "dark", harmful, perhaps even evil. The
worm might even be read as a kind of phallic symbol, with
the whole poem becoming a disturbing metaphor for the
loss of sexual innocence.

   With our momentum behind this reading, the ways
in which the rose itself is described also start to cast a different shadow. As we initially noted, "sick" seems to mean
damaged, or harmed – but it is not a word we would normally apply to a flower. Once again, it implies a much
more human condition. This is supported by the reference
to "joy" in line six, an emotion with distinctively human
associations (perhaps spiritual; perhaps sexual). The rose's
"bed" that the worm has found out can, of course, be seen
simply as a flowerbed – but it might also indicate the "bed"
of a human lover. With all these suggestions of threatening sexual force suddenly looming in the poem, we could
be forgiven for thinking that this "Rose", capitalised by
Blake, is not in fact a flower at all, but actually is a girl's

name. An even darker reading begins to take shape: perhaps Rose is "sick", her "life" destroyed, because she has just been infected with venereal disease by this mysterious and destructive male presence (syphilis, as it happens, was especially common in Blake's time).

Where does this all leave us? Is this, in the end, a nature poem about a dying flower – or is it a dark metaphor for sexual loss of innocence? The key point is that these questions *do not need* an answer. We do not need to make up our minds. In fact, a good reading of this poem *depends* upon us not making up our minds. The poem does not have a single "answer" that we need to access. Both our readings are equally valid and true. This is the crucial truth about ambiguity in poetry. Uncertainty is a good thing – when reading poems, uncertainty is our friend. The right way to read this poem, or any poem in fact, is to look actively for these ambiguities – moments that seem strange, or confusing, or that seem open to various conflicting interpretations. We can then *write* about these conflicts in our response. Instead of becoming the core of our frustration – a barrier to understanding or writing about a poem – they can become the core material of our essay. There is no need at all to come to any conclusion about which interpretation might be "correct". In many ways, what makes a poem interesting is the simultaneous presence of these various threads of meaning; it is not the job of the reader to "solve" or "answer" the poem, but instead to point out how all these different meanings and possible interpretations coexist.

Case Study in Ambiguity #2: John Donne

Throughout the history of English poetry, we find poets exploring and utilising various different kinds of ambiguity. Whether this relates to ambiguities in the meanings of words, or in subject matter and themes, or in tone, poets are very often in the business of actively exploring uncertainties within how language might be used. One great exponent of ambiguity was John Donne, the early seventeenth-century poet, whose work swings wildly from innuendo-riddled erotic verse to earnest devotional poems (and sometimes, indeed, both at the same time). Many of his poems crackle with the coexistence of deeply conflicting, contradictory moods and perspectives. One of his late religious poems, entitled "A Hymn to God the Father", begins as follows:

> Wilt thou forgive that sin where I begun,
>   Which was my sin, though it were done before?
> Wilt thou forgive that sin, through which I run,
>   And do run still, though still I do deplore?
>   When thou hast done, thou hast not done,
>   For I have more.

This poem seems, at first, to be a straightforward appeal to God for forgiveness. The speaker worries about the "sin" of which he is now guilty, and of which he has been guilty in the past; worse, though, is that he "run[s] still" through the same sin, unable to stop himself. The speaker may be referring to a specific sin here, but the lack of clarification seems to suggest that "sin" describes a general sinfulness of character.

This simple reading of religious supplication is complicated, though, once we notice what is happening in the last two lines of this stanza. "When thou hast done, thou hast not done" ... our poet's name, remember, is John *Donne*. A pun is being made here on the words "done" and "Donne". The poet seems to be playfully suggesting that, when God might have *Donne* – in the sense of securing his soul – in fact God "hast not Donne", since our poet has "more" sins up his sleeve, rendering the destiny of his soul in doubt once more. The wordplay is given an additional dimension when we discover that Donne's wife's name was Anne *More* – "When thou hast done, thou hast not done,/ For I have <u>more</u>". If "more" here refers to his wife, Anne More, then the line seems to suggest that the poet's human love and desire for his wife competes with, and conflicts with, his love for God.

What are we to make of this wordplay, in a poem that seems on the surface to be so seriously focused on sin and forgiveness? This has been a topic of great debate amongst scholars of Donne's work. Some have said that the puns seem to undermine the seriousness of the poem's surface meaning. What choice are we to make? Is this a serious poem appealing for divine forgiveness, or is it a playful, mischievous example of Donne's wit, rich with clever wordplay? The answer, once again, is that we do not have to choose. The poem is *both these things at the same time* – the wordplay *coexists* with the emotional torture of the poet's awareness of sin, but does not cancel it out. Once again, we have two avenues of interpretation available to us. The right way to approach an analytical response is to focus not on one of them, but on both. In poetry, ambiguity is always there to be embraced.

Poetry Unlocked: The Treasure of Ambiguity

Let us return to the situation described at the beginning of the chapter. A student staring at a poem, confused and frustrated, unsure about where to begin. The place to begin, I want to suggest, is right in the middle of precisely that confusion which can feel so much like a stumbling block. The secret is to *use* the confusion you might feel when a piece of language looks like it could be interpreted in two, three, or more different ways. This is the treasure of ambiguity – and it is at the heart of thinking about, and writing about poetry. Way, way back, in 1930, William Empson argued that "the machinations of ambiguity are among the very roots of poetry". Ambiguity, in other words, is at the heart of poems – and by extension, it needs to be at the heart of how we read poems. The environment and culture surrounding classroom – and even, sometimes, university – study can pressurise us into thinking that there are clearly defined answers to every task we must complete. With poetry, more than any other form of writing, this simply isn't so. The key is to become *comfortable* with the uncertainty of multiple meanings existing all at the same time. When writing about poems, ambiguity is the treasure at the heart of everything. Master this, and everything else will follow.

What Do Poems Mean?

Why Poems Get Written

It is not a question that is very often asked. When a student has a poem placed under their nose for consideration, it can often feel like the poem has floated into existence out of thin air, or like it has been taken by the teacher from some secret teachers' vault of classroom poems. The question of why the poem was written in the first place does not tend to get much of a look in. It doesn't really matter, after all, does it? What matters is what the cursed thing means. For many students, the actual *reasons* for a poem's existence either have no significance or get lost in the pressurised fog of classroom study. When the aims of poetry do get considered, it can too often lead to the worst conclusion of all: that poems have in some way been written *in order to be studied in the classroom* – that their function is to be analysed and decoded for essay or examination purposes.

When thinking about and writing about a poem, then, it is always worth considering *why* the poet bothered to write that particular poem at all. It leads to a very important, oft-ignored point: that a poet will always have had some sort of significant reason to sit down and write the thing you are staring at and trying to understand. Writing poems is a time-consuming business. Whatever motivated the author to sit down and write, it must have been significant enough to generate the effort needed to write the poem. The poet must have had something they wanted to say. The poem must *mean* something: it must have some message, or a series of messages, that the poet wants the reader to understand.

In the last chapter, of course, I attempted to explain that trying to look for an "answer" to a poem is not the best way of reading it. Poems often explore things like contradiction, paradox, and mystery. As such, we should never try to "solve" a poem by saying it is definitively about one particular thing. The poet Anne Stevenson has argued that "poetry differs from prose in being more than *about* a subject". As such, poetry is rather like music: the words of poems "signify feelings and impressions that are not translatable out of the words and cadences in which they appear". Her message here about the mystery of poetry is clear enough. This does not, though, particularly help us to find a constructive approach to the academic study of poems. After all, a poem will never have been written with no meaning at all. It will always have been intended to express *something*. Moreover, it will not usually just have a simple or shallow meaning. A poem about picking strawberries, for instance, will not usually just be about picking strawberries – if it was, why would the poet bother to write it?

As it happens, there is a poem that illustrates precisely this point using precisely this example. It is by Emily Dickinson, and runs as follows:

> Over the fence –
> Strawberries – grow –
> Over the fence –
> I could climb – if I tried, I know –
> Berries are nice!
>
> But – if I stained my Apron –
> God would certainly scold!
> Oh, dear, I guess if he were a Boy –
> He'd – climb – if He could!

Emily Dickinson was writing in the late nineteenth century, and is now considered to be one of the greatest of all American poets. In her lifetime, though, she was little recognised, and published almost nothing. The eccentric punctuation here – with mostly dashes use to punctuate the lines – is characteristic of her verse, which exists mostly in manuscript form. Some early critics took the view that her poems should be "regularised" into more orthodox punctuation, but this is now widely seen as unnecessary and damaging. The dashes are a crucial part of the essence of the verse, creating a uniquely disrupted, unstable quality to our reading of each poem.

This short poem by Dickinson seems at first to be light-hearted, even trivial. The opening stanza describes a simple yearning for the strawberries – the repetition of "over the fence" underlines the speaker's frustrated inability to get at them. It is a basic, even childish desire; the line "Berries are nice!" heightens this sense of childishness, suggesting this is either a childhood memory or that the speaker of the poem is actually a child. Is the poem really, though, simply about wanting to pick some strawberries? The content of the second stanza, in particular, creates a feeling that this is not *quite* a fully adequate explanation of the poem.

　　Once again, elements of the poem's language pull us, as readers, towards other meanings that might sit alongside the simple surface meaning we most quickly notice. Dickinson mentions being "scold[ed]" by God if she were to stain her apron – a fear of chastisement from a source of traditional authority. The imagining of God as a "boy" seems to bring to the poem a deeper, more serious concern with gender power relations. If God were a boy, he would wish to climb the tree, at the same time as rebuking the female speaker for her apparently unfeminine ambitions. The "apron" of the first stanza might now be looked at as an emblem of the imposition of domestic expectations. The fence of the opening lines now reads as not only a literal fence, but also a metaphor for the suffocating social restrictions and limitations imposed on women in late nineteenth-century America.

　　One useful way of thinking about the multiple meanings of poetry is through the idea of a "surface meaning" and a "deeper meaning". A poem will always, of course, have some sort of "surface meaning". In fact, this might often seem, to students, to be something strangely minor or unimportant: a leaf fluttering to the ground, or a door opening, or the moment rain begins, that sort of thing. Looking at the surface meaning, it can raise the question of why the poet bothered to write the poem. In the case of Dickinson's poem, the surface meaning is that it describes a desire to pick some strawberries. At a surface level, poems often seem to describe fleeting, seemingly insignificant moments like this. It can, in such situations, be a good move to think *there must be something more here*. If the surface meaning seems superficial, inconsequential – what might the poem really be about, under the surface? Are there clues that might lead you to something deeper? This is another wonderful way of unlocking the door of poetry – opening up levels of depth, and sophistication, that might become the building blocks of an excellent essay response.

"The Forge": A Case Study in Deep Meaning

In order to explore this idea of "deep meaning" in poetry, I want to take a poem by Seamus Heaney – one of the great English-language poets of the last fifty years, and frequently the object of study for secondary and university students. It is entitled "The Forge", and runs as follows:

> All I know is a door into the dark.
> Outside, old axles and iron hoops rusting;

> Inside, the hammered anvil's short-pitched ring,
> The unpredictable fantail of sparks
> Or hiss when a new shoe toughens in water.
> The anvil must be somewhere in the centre,
> Horned as a unicorn, at one end square,
> Set there immoveable: an altar
> Where he expends himself in shape and music.
> Sometimes, leather-aproned, hairs in his nose,
> He leans out on the jamb, recalls a clatter
> Of hoofs where traffic is flashing in rows;
> Then grunts and goes in, with a slam and flick
> To beat real iron out, to work the bellows.

Let's begin by asking the simple question, "What is this poem about?" At a surface level, the poem seems to describe someone working at an "anvil". We might know the name for someone who makes this work his trade: a *blacksmith*. The poem describes a blacksmith. The "forge" of the title is, therefore, the furnace in which he heats his metals. The "new shoe" in the fifth line must be a horseshoe. This is our "surface meaning" for the poem – it is about a blacksmith going about his daily work.

Much of the language Heaney uses in the course of describing this blacksmith's activity is quite forceful and masculine. References to the "hammered anvil" and a new shoe that "toughens" create a vivid sense of powerful, manual labour; towards the end of the poem, the onomatopoeic monosyllables "slam", "flick" and "beat" have an especially punchy effect. The blacksmith himself, "leather-aproned, hairs in his nose", is presented as a figure of almost cartoonish, brutish strength – he doesn't speak in the poem, with the only sound he makes being a bestial "grunt". Alongside the primal potency of the blacksmith is also a sense, in various places, that he is evocative of some bygone age. The references to "old axles" and "iron hoops" suggest a distinctly old-fashioned atmosphere. Towards the end of the poem, leaning out from his workshop, he "recalls a clatter/ Of hoofs where traffic is flashing in rows": the reference here to "traffic" heavily implies the car traffic of the contemporary world, in contrast to the "hoofs" of horses and carts that he recalls in his mind, the long-gone traffic of yesteryear. The blacksmith becomes a point of connection to this lost world of the past: his "grunt" before turning away from the traffic and going back inside perhaps indicates not just his primal animal strength, but also his sneering disapproval of the high-tech, post-industrial world he sees outside.

In addition, a reader paying attention to the *form* of the poem – the topic of our next chapter – might notice that this is a sonnet. Traditionally, sonnets are fourteen-line poems with particular rhyme schemes, written in rhythmically undulating ten-syllable lines known as "iambic pentameter": the intricacy of the form has often involved association with harmony, and balance. A careful reader might note, though, that this poem is a particularly rough-edged sonnet; it is fourteen lines, like a traditional sonnet, but the rhythm and metre of each line is very variable, often not seeming regular at all. Many of the rhymes, too – rusting/ring, centre/square, music/clatter/flick – are not consistent or full rhymes. The shape of the poem, in other words – a notably rough-around-the-edges approach to a traditionally intricate and harmonious form – might help to reflect the rough-edged forcefulness of the blacksmith and what he is designed to represent.

Broadly speaking, this all seems simple enough. Here is our poem about a blacksmith. But *why*, exactly, did Heaney write it? Is it enough to say that he simply wanted to describe a blacksmith at his work – giving a sense, as he did so, of how this is an old-fashioned practice, in danger of dying out completely? This seems like an admirable enough reason, perhaps, and therefore like a reasonable enough theory for why the poem was written. But it doesn't *quite* provide the "deep meaning" that might fully satisfy us as a reader. Sure, the poem is about a blacksmith. But is that all there is to it? Where is the "deep meaning" here?

When we look closely, we might notice that various details in the language of the poem seem strange, tricky to work out, and certainly not consistent with the straightforward interpretation on which we have settled. The first line, for instance, is very odd. "All I know is a door into the dark". What happens to the speaker here – the first-person voice, the "I" in "All I know" – in the rest of the poem? After this first line, it seems mysteriously to disappear; the rest of the poem reads as a third-person description of the blacksmith. In addition, there are aspects of the way the blacksmith's work is described that sit uneasily with the emphasis on brute force that we have already identified. The anvil is given a kind of mythological and religious significance – compared to a "unicorn", and then in the following line described as an "altar". The blacksmith expends himself in "shape and music"; these words don't suggest something manual and physical so much as something *artistic* and *imaginative*. At this moment in the poem, the description sounds less like someone making a horseshoe, and more like someone making a piece of art – more, we might even say, like someone making poetry. A connection is forged, and the poem sparks with new life: this blacksmith is a creator, an *artist*, just like the poet who is describing him.

Here, we have the "deep meaning" which we seek. The blacksmith becomes something much more than a blacksmith. He becomes an emblem of creativity. For all the roughness and force of his work, he is *creating* something in his forge, and Heaney is building a bridge, as a result, between the blacksmith and the figure of the poet. "All I know is a door into the dark" … the first line reads now like the poet entering through a door into the darkness of his own imagination – a space in which he conjures the image of the blacksmith, who is himself conjuring the horseshoe in an act of both physical power and creative energy. The "forge" becomes both the literal forge in which the blacksmith moulds his iron, and a metaphorical forge of the imagination, the space in which the poet can create his poetry. Once we have accessed this level to the poem, it very much becomes a poem of "deep meaning" – a metaphorical poem in which the blacksmith becomes an expression of the mysterious forces of artistic creation. Once again, the moments of strangeness in the poem's language become the key moments for us, allowing us to leap from a simple or superficial level of interpretation into something deeper, more sophisticated, and more meaningful.

What's in a Title?

This reading of Heaney's poem, exploring it in terms of a "surface meaning" and a "deep meaning", provides one useful model for how we might approach the analysis of other poems. It can be very useful to have some "ways in" to a poem – some strategies that we can call upon in order to get started with our analytical thinking. In this case, we have several questions in our armoury that could be applied to a poem. *What is the poem about? What is its surface meaning? What is its deep meaning?* In our reading above, the "forge" of the title ends up crackling with various meanings, implying not only a literal forge but also a forge of the imagination, the creative generator from which all art, including poetry, is birthed. As a result, the building blocks of a sophisticated analytical response float into view.

That particular title, "The Forge", looks at first glance like a pretty unexciting title. It seems just to be descriptive in a one-dimensional way; only on a close reading of the poem does it open up with interest value. Titles to poems, I want to suggest, often work in this sort of way. We might often skim over a title. It might seem like it has a fairly functional role – giving the reader an initial indication of a poem's subject matter, before we get into the serious business of reading and analysing the poem itself. What I want to suggest here is that a careful consideration of a poem's title can not only be an extremely useful starting point to thinking about a poem – it can actually *influence* our understanding of poems in ways that, without the title, we would not be able to access.

As an example, I want to take a poem by Stephen Spender. For the moment I will deliberately refrain from revealing the poem's title. The poem begins as follows:

> My parents kept me from children who were rough
> Who threw words like stones and wore torn clothes
> Their thighs showed through rags they ran in the street
> And climbed cliffs and stripped by the country streams.

If we once again apply our initial question, "What's this poem about?", the simple answer is that it seems to describe a young child who is the victim of bullying by other local children. These "rough" children live a more physical, active existence that the speaker of the poem seems to envy – they are able to "climb cliffs" and to strip their clothes off by "country streams", accessing a kind of primal oneness with the natural world. They are strong, too; in the second stanza of the poem, they are described as possessing "muscles like iron", whilst in contrast, the speaker has a "lisp" and seems physically weak. He appears to be physically bullied by these other children ("their knees tight on my arms"), as well as being mocked by them for his lisp. The final line of the poem seems to underline that it is, fundamentally, a poem of resentment: "I longed to forgive them but they never smiled". Whilst envying their life, the speaker feels bitterness towards these other children as a result of their harsh treatment of him. As a result, he is unable to find forgiveness for them in his heart.

The major focus of this poem seems, in other words, to be on these other children who treat the speaker so harshly and seem to cause him bitterness and misery. How is my point about title relevant to this? Well, Spender's title for this poem is "My Parents". Let us consider this for a moment. It looks, at first glance, like a strange title for the poem. The description is, mostly, of the "rough" children, and the speaker's experiences of them. The speaker's *parents* are only referenced in the poem's opening line – they begin the poem, then they disappear. Or *do* they? Spender's decision to call the poem "My Parents" invites us to consider the possibility that the parents in this poem are more significant than we might initially think. It might, for example, be useful for us to look again at the sense of *envy* the speaker seems to express for these strong other children, who are able to live a freer, more physically active and dynamic life. Those opening words of the poem – "My parents kept me" – contain an ambiguity. The word "kept" might convey a sense of protection – the parents kept him protected from these rough, unpleasant, dangerous children. But "kept" also has associations of entrapment, of imprisonment. Perhaps, in fact, the speaker's resentment isn't simply directed towards these other children: it is directed at *his own parents*, for keeping him back from a life of vibrant physical activity that, without their controlling presence, he might have been able to access. The final line – "I longed to forgive them, but they never smiled" – might not actually refer to the other children. It *may* refer, instead, to the speaker's own parents. He is unable to forgive them for the upbringing they enforced upon him, consigning him to a life of restricted, physically weak withdrawal from the other children around him as he grew up. This reading of Spender's poem, closely focusing on the title he chose, is a great example of how useful and beneficial titles can be as we read and analyse poetry. There is almost always something to say about a title. Even when a title looks straightforward, simple, and obvious, they usually have something more to tell us, suggesting possible ideas and meanings that we might otherwise miss. And in the case of "My Parents", the title doesn't just provide us with some useful ideas to consider – it actually *changes* our reading of the entire poem.

By approaching poems from these various angles, what we are developing is a series of strategies for reading. A kind of toolkit, we might say, that will allow us to analyse poems with security and confidence. In the last chapter, I focused on how the ambiguity of poetry can be a friend not an enemy, allowing us to avoid any oversimplified efforts to "solve" a poem's meaning. In this chapter, by focusing on the "surface" and "deep" meanings of poems as well as on the significance of titles, I have similarly attempted to provide some practical "ways in" to the analysis of poetry. By keeping in mind these straightforward practical ideas, my hope is that the ultimate horror situation in studying English – of staring at a poem in frustrated confusion, unable to get started, unable to respond – can reliably be avoided.

The Challenge of Poetic Form

What is "Poetic Form"?

I began this book by claiming that, of all forms of writing that students have to study in English, poetry is most often the most difficult. In fifteen years of teaching literature at university and secondary level, I am very confident that this is accurate. But *within the context* of studying poetry, there is one area that is usually more challenging than anything else: poetic form. When asked to consider or analyse "form" in poems, students often find it hard to know where to start. It can be tempting, in such situations, to reduce poems to a kind of elaborate technical exercise. Under pressure to find *something* to say, students can too often fall into the cardinal sin of "feature spotting" – simply *identifying* the aspects of form in a poem rather than actually *analysing* them or connecting them to the poem's meaning. In other words – as the most difficult element of the most difficult form of writing in the subject of English – the question of poetic form, and how to analyse it, is a serious one that demands very careful attention.

We might sensibly start with a simple question – what *is* poetic form, exactly? To answer this, let us start with what seems to be a very straightforward sentence:

> Today I went out to the shops, and bought a loaf of bread.

We have here thirteen words, delivered in what feels like a fairly clear, basic fashion. Written out like this, we would call this a sentence of *prose*. All this really means is language written in sentences as we would normally encounter them in stories, articles, news features, novels, biographies, and the like. Most writing is in prose. This book is in prose, for example. Though it might be a crude way of putting it, it is nevertheless quite useful to think of "prose" as essentially signifying "normal" writing, in the various forms this can take.

So what is different, exactly, about poetry? A good starting point might be to think of poetry as a form of writing in which some attention has been paid to how it is *shaped*, or arranged. Let us consider this reconfigured version of the same simple sentence:

> Today I went
> out to the shops and
>
> bought a loaf
> of bread.

Or this one:

> Today I
>   went out

> to the shops
>   and bought
>   a
>   loaf of bread.

Or this one:

> Today I went out to the shops,
> And bought a loaf of bread.

All of these versions share one thing: that the writer (me in this case) has paid some attention to *where* the words should go on the page. The words don't just run to the right-hand margin of the page, as happens in prose. The right-hand edge breaks off, deliberately – at different places in each of these versions. The sentence is written out in *lines*: four lines, in version one; six lines, in version two; two lines, in version three. We call this writing in *verse* rather than in prose. Fundamentally, a good basic way of thinking about poetry, as distinct from prose, is this idea of considering not just what words might be used, but also where they might be put, and how they might relate to each other. *Poetic form*, then, is simply what particular arrangement, what particular shape, the words of a poem might have been given on the page as you read it. There are various dimensions to this notion of the shaping or arranging of words, and the first one I wish to explore is especially well known – familiar to pretty much everyone, in fact, right from their very earliest experiments with language and sound patterns as young children. This is the phenomenon of *rhyme*.

The Reasons for Rhyme

Not all poems rhyme. No one says that they must. Back in
the seventeenth century, John Milton was already rebel-
ling against the presence of rhyme in English poetry; he
rather dismissively described it as "the jingling sound of
like endings, a fault avoyded by the learned Ancients both
in Poetry and all good Oratory". Since the beginning of
the twentieth century, in particular, many poets have tried
to avoid a reliance on rhyme in favour of more innovative
and original methods. Nevertheless, rhyme remains one of
the most conspicuous features of poetry, one of the easiest,
clearest ways that a poem becomes identifiable as a poem.
However, the question of *why* poets use rhyme – of its
purpose, its *effect* – is not so commonly considered, and
not so straightforward. Simply pointing out that a poem
either rhymes or does not rhyme does not get us very far.
We need to consider carefully the reasons why rhyme might
be used, the effect it creates when it appears, and the best
possible ways to approach the analysis of rhyme in poetry.

So, why rhyme at all? The use of rhyme is related to
long-held connections between poetry and song. Rhyme
is, effectively, a form of music. It is the chiming of word-
sounds together, and as such, it might be fair to say that
moments of rhyme are where language is at its most musi-
cal. The potential effects of rhyme, though, are somewhat
complicated and unpredictable. These can vary greatly,
often depending on the overall tone or subject matter

of the particular poem. Rhyme often seems to reflect or reinforce elements of a poem's overall message. A good example, once again, is William Blake – whose *Songs of Innocence and of Experience* express a vast and complex range of emotions and moods, from outright joy to rage, anger, and despair. Here are the opening lines of his poem, "The Ecchoing Green":

> The sun does arise,
> And make happy the skies.
> The merry bells ring
> To welcome the Spring.
> The sky-lark and thrush,
> The birds of the bush,
> Sing louder around,
> To the bells' cheerful sound.
> While our sports shall be seen
> On the Ecchoing Green.

This poem celebrates both the beauty of nature and also, as it goes on, the people of various generations who laugh and play on this particular "green". Its tone is one of happiness, positivity, and joy. The language is simple and childlike, but the rhyme is also a key part of the upbeat tone. It is written in pairs of rhyming lines – what we call *rhyming couplets*. This heavy use of rhyme helps, here, to create a songlike feel – a sense of overarching harmony and unity. The short lines, too – just five or six syllables in each – help to emphasise the rhyme even further. In this poem, in other words, the poet's conspicuous use of rhyme heightens the atmosphere of optimistic celebration that the poem describes.

In contrast, these are the opening lines of another poem from Blake's *Songs*, entitled "London":

> I wander thro' each charter'd street,
> Near where the charter'd Thames does flow.
> And mark in every face I meet
> Marks of weakness, marks of woe.

In this poem, Blake is setting a very different mood, raging against the oppression and the social injustice he witnessed in late eighteenth-century London. It is a poem of political anger and protest – not, in this case, a poem of celebration at all. And yet we notice that there is rhyme here, too: alternate rhyme, rather than couplets, but still very much a conspicuous element of the poem. We cannot claim here that the rhyme creates any real sense of optimism. Instead, it seems to enforce the sense of monotony and entrapment that the poem describes – part of the suffocating feel of the poem. The rhyme, in other words, once again reflects the poem's subject matter, which here could not be much more different to the subject matter of "The Ecchoing Green". The contrasting tones of Blake's poems provide a perfect example of why we cannot oversimplify rhyme as providing one specific, particular effect in poetry.

We do, in other words, need to be careful that we are thinking about rhyme in a sensitive way, always linking it to what a poem describes rather than presuming it will always have the same kind of effect every time. Having said this, there is a single basic quality to rhyme which feels inescapably true, whatever the specifics of a poem's content:

there must always be *something* harmonising about the presence of rhyme in poetry. It is, after all, the bringing together of language via the chiming of sound. Even in Blake's "London", the sense of oppression that the rhyme helps to convey still stems from its regularising, unifying quality. Rhyme, we might say, is a force that holds its gaze in the direction of harmony and order, rather than the opposite. This very fact is one of the reasons why some poets have at times rebelled against it. Wilfred Owen, perhaps the most celebrated poet of the First World War, sometimes erred away from full rhyme in favour of half rhymes, as in his famous poem "Strange Meeting":

> It seemed that out of battle I escaped
> Down some profound dull tunnel, long since scooped
> Through granites which titanic wars had groined.
>
> Yet also there encumbered sleepers groaned,
> Too fast in thought or death to be bestirred.
> Then, as I probed them, one sprang up, and stared

In this poem, the speaker is a soldier who has just died and has entered a kind of dark underworld, only to encounter someone who turns out to be an enemy soldier he had killed ("I am the enemy you killed, my friend. I knew you in this dark ..."). Owen's poetry tends to be energised by deep rage and despair about the awfulness and the violence of war. As such, he felt that, sometimes, rhyme simply was not appropriate – its chiming music was simply inconsistent with the horrors he wished to describe. The half rhyme of "Strange Meeting" – escape/scooped, groined/groaned, and so on – is a deliberate move to avoid what he saw as the upbeat musicality of rhyme in favour of a more sombre, downbeat tone.

So: rhyme is music, a quality that brings harmony to the sounds of words, harking back to the ancient connections between poetry and song. But there are other resonances to rhyme, too. For example, it is worth looking out for occasions where the poet might be playing around with the words he chooses to rhyme with each other. Poets are often being very deliberate and careful with such choices, making links and connections via the rhyming of particular words. There are many examples of this, but to take one, here is the opening of a famous poem by Lord Byron called "She Walks in Beauty":

> She walks in beauty, like the night
> Of cloudless climes and starry skies;
> And all that's best of dark and bright
> Meet in her aspect and her eyes;
> Thus mellowed to that tender light
> Which heaven to gaudy day denies.

These opening lines all focus on the extraordinary beauty of the woman Byron wants to describe (the story behind it is that Byron saw a woman by the name of Anne Beatrix Wilmot at a ball, and was so struck by her beauty that he wrote this poem about her the next morning). The nature of his description focuses on a combination of darkness and brightness in her appearance. When we look at the use of rhyme, it becomes clear that this tangled sense of light and dark is at work there, too, woven into the fabric of the rhyme itself. Byron ends the first line with the word "night"; the two words with which it rhymes, in this stanza, are "bright" and "light". The rhyme *fuses together* this sense of light and dark, complementing and enforcing the nature of the physical description. This technique, of choosing rhyming words that might link together in a network of descriptive or thematic significance, can be thought of as another dimension to the basic unifying effect of rhyme. Rhyme is harmony, unity, and connection – not simply the "jangling sound of like endings" that Milton dismissed it as, but a place where meanings can come together, merging in the alchemy of word-sounds.

Measuring Rhythms: The Importance of Metre

All language has rhythm. The particular sound patterns and weightings of different languages greatly vary, but the patterns are always there. In the English language, we tend to register these patterns in terms of "stress"; more precisely, in poetry, we identify and measure which syllables are stressed, or emphasised, within words and sentences. Let us take, for instance, a simple statement: "I brushed my teeth as usual this morning". If we pay some attention to the rhythm of syllables here, and note which ones are naturally *emphasised*, a pattern quickly becomes clear. "I **brushed** my **teeth** as **us**ual this **morn**ing". <u>Brushed</u> is a stressed syllable, as is <u>teeth</u>, as is the first syllable of <u>usual</u>, and the first syllable of <u>morn</u>ing. These are just the syllables that we *naturally* stress as we sound out or speak these words (try sounding out the same sentence, stressing only the syllables <u>my</u>, <u>as</u>, and <u>this</u> – you'll see how unnatural and difficult this feels). When talking about "metre" in poetry, all that is really meant is how the natural stress rhythms of the language might be measured. Careful poets pay careful attention to every element of the language they use, including its rhythm; how the rhythm is organised – the metre of the poem – can form a significant part of a poem's overall meaning and effect.

There are many different ways in which poets use metre, but the best place for us to start is with iambic metre. This is, by a very long way, the most common metre in English poetry. It is made up of individual iambs, a term that refers to a two-syllable unit whereby the stress falls on the second syllable: de-**DUM**. Examples of iambic individual words in English are to**day**, re**fer**, lam**ent**, a**gain**, en**ough**. You will notice, as you read these words, that the stress clearly and naturally falls on the second syllable as we pronounce them: it really doesn't work to attempt a pronunciation of **TO**-day, for instance, with the stress on the first syllable. The word is iambic. And iambic metre has, for centuries, been the cornerstone of English poetry, for the simple reason that it naturally and easily fits with the stress patterns of the English language. It doesn't take too much work to organise words in the English language iambically. This sentence is a great example, actually. (Look again: This **sent**ence **is** a **great** exam**ple**, **actually**. Note how the natural stress falls on every other syllable as we read it).

Poetry organised in iambic metre has a long history in English poetry. We even find it if we look all the way back to Geoffrey Chaucer, the most significant pioneer of English language poetry in the fourteenth century:

> When **that** Ap**rille** **with** his **shou**res **soote**
> The **droghte** of **March** hath **perc**ed **to** the **roote**

> (Note: in fourteenth-century English, the "e" of "Aprille", and the second syllables of "shoures" and "perced", would have been actively sounded out.)

These lines show how Chaucer had already worked out that an iambic metre would work especially well as a means of rhythmically organising his poetry. Chaucer's lines are in *iambic pentameter* – five iambs in each line, and so ten syllables in total. Over the centuries this remained the most popular manifestation of iambic metre in English, but iambic line lengths can vary: *iambic tetrameter* is eight-syllable lines (four iambs), *iambic trimeter* is six-syllable lines (three iambs). Lines longer or shorter than these do sometimes crop up, but they are pretty rare.

What, though, is the *effect* of writing in such a metre? What makes it significantly distinct from the natural rhythms of prose? This is not an easy question – and part of the answer, for poets across the centuries, will have been connected more to convention than to a conscious desire to create a particular effect. To some extent, the use of a regular metre in poetry is a signal that the writing is poetry – written in verse, and not in prose. A little like with rhyme, though, the basic effect of using a *regular* metre in poetry is the creation of harmony. Let us go back to "She Walks in Beauty" by Byron:

> She walks in beauty, like the night
> Of cloudless climes and starry skies

Byron is basing his metre here, quite clearly, on iambic tetrameter: eight-syllable lines of alternate stresses. The regularity of this metre seems to fit with the beauty of the woman he describes, and the unity of elements of dark and bright that he notes in her appearance. We might say, in other words, that the regular nature of the metre fits with the tone and the content of what the poem describes.

Having said this, the idea of metre as a harmonising force has quite serious limitations. Are all poems written in iambic metre about something harmonious? The answer, of course, is no. Moreover, any effort to write a *purely* iambic poem, with absolutely no variation at all, is likely to lead to something very monotonous and dull. Most poems, even if they are based in, say, iambic metre, are *not* consistently iambic all the way through. Poets are often in the business of manipulating particular rhythms in particular lines, in order to highlight or emphasise particular ideas. It is, in other words, often more useful to look for changes in the metre – *disruptions* to the overall pattern – rather than focusing on the more crude question of whether a poem is, for instance, iambic or not. Alfred, Lord Tennyson – one of the great poets of the Victorian era, and poet laureate from 1850 to 1892 – wrote a long poem, "In Memoriam", in the wake of the death of his close friend Arthur Hallam. In it, he expounds at length on the grief and sadness he feels at the loss of his friend. Some famous lines run as follows:

> He is not here; but far away
> The noise of life begins again,
> And ghastly thro' the drizzling rain
> On the bald street breaks the blank day.

Note here, first of all, that Tennyson is using a base of iambic tetrameter for his poem – exactly the same metre that Byron uses in "She Walks in Beauty". After three reasonably regular iambic lines, though, we are given something much more jarring. "On the bald street breaks the blank day". Tennyson is describing the coming of a new day – but it is a bleak and empty one, "ghastly" as a result of his great friend's absence. The description of what should traditionally be a positive, optimistic moment – the breaking of dawn – is instead described as "blank", with the street itself "bald", both of these words conveying a sense of emptiness and loss. In terms of metre, Tennyson further emphasises the emotional turbulence he wishes to convey by delivering a very rhythmically irregular line: "On the **bald street breaks** the **blank day**". This is not iambic at all; instead of syllables two, four, six and eight being stressed, the stress lands on syllables three, four, five, seven and eight.

The striking irregularity enforces the overall sense of emotional disharmony and trauma here, also highlighted by the harsh alliteration of "b" sounds and the use of entirely monosyllabic words in the line. It is a great example, in other words, of how a poet *disrupts* the overarching metre in order to create a particular effect.

Another useful example of the careful manipulation of rhythm can be found in a famous sonnet by Elizabeth Barrett Browning, which begins as follows:

> How do I love thee? Let me count the ways.
> I love thee to the depth and breadth and height
> My soul can reach, when feeling out of sight
> For the ends of being and ideal grace.

These lines, for the most part, feel harmoniously iambic. Indeed, Browning seems to be using this iambic base in order deliberately to emphasise the various dimensions of the speaker's love – note where the stresses fall in "I **love** thee to the **depth** and **breadth** and **height**/ My **soul** can **reach**". This simple reading would link the harmony of the speaker's love to the harmonious nature of the iambic metre. If we look again at those opening words, though – "How do I love thee?" – they don't quite work iambically. The *first* syllable appears to be stressed ("**How** do I love thee?"). The whole poem, in other words, begins with a disruption to the iambic pentameter base that Browning is broadly deploying. This *could* lead us to a competing point about the intense emotion of the speaker, here, in these lines. At once we have a more sophisticated reading of the metre and how Browning is using it: alongside the generally iambic framework, suggestive of harmony and unity, we have a moment of disrupted rhythm right at the start of the opening line that might suggest the *spontaneity* and *fervour* of the speaker's passion.

What we are moving towards, in this example, is a more *precise* – and therefore more useful – consideration of poets' use of metre. Noticing whether or not a poem is based around iambic metre does not really get us very far (you will remember I said something very similar with regard to rhyme). Good poets are often subtly *manipulating* the metre throughout a poem, creating shifts and changes that are much more productive material for potential analysis. Another significant poet of the First World War was Siegfried Sassoon; like Owen, he wrote passionately and angrily about the awfulness and violence he witnessed on the battlefield. Sassoon's poem "Attack" describes a group of soldiers going "over the top" – the poem's title becomes ironic as, rather than attacking anything, the soldiers stagger forwards into their inevitable death:

> The barrage roars and lifts. Then, clumsily bowed
> With bombs and guns and shovels and battle-gear,
> Men jostle and climb to meet the bristling fire.

Sassoon's metrical basis in this poem is iambic pentameter. Notice, though, that as soon as he begins to describe the soldiers and their movements as they "attack", the metre becomes more clumsy and irregular, incorporating disruptions to the iambic metrical base: "**clum**sily **bowed**/ With **bombs** and **guns** and **shov**els and **battl**e-gear". The effect of this irregularity is to highlight the awkwardness – and, therefore, the vulnerability – of these soldiers. Weighed down by all their gear, they become sitting ducks for enemy gunfire. These lines are another good example of how the poet has carefully *manipulated* his metre, at a particular point, in order to emphasise some element of the picture he is endeavouring to present.

A Word About Other Metres

By no means is it the case that all English poetry is in iambic metre. I am, instead, paying particular attention to it here because it is so common – in the course of reading and studying poems, you will inevitably encounter plenty of poems that have iambic metre as their base. Other metrical choices are rather less widespread – but they do crop up, and some are worth a particular mention. Tennyson's poem "The Charge of the Light Brigade" begins as follows:

Half a league, half a league,
Half a league onward,
All in the valley of Death
  Rode the six hundred.

Tennyson's aim here is to present the drama, action, and chaos of the battlefield, as he describes a group of cavalry bravely charging against the Russian army in the Crimean War. In order to accentuate this atmosphere, he chooses a metre built mostly out of *dactyls* – a three-syllable foot where only the first is stressed. The rhythm created – "**Half** a league, **half** a league, **Half** a league **on**ward" – is fast paced, resembling, we might say, the sound and the speed of the charging horses. This sense of pace is created through the fact that, in this metrical pattern, the majority of syllables are *unstressed* rather than stressed – meaning that the lines read more rapidly. Compare it with the very slow, halting line we highlighted from "In Memoriam" – "On the **bald street breaks** the **blank day**" – where five of the eight syllables are stressed, *slowing down* our reading of the line. In "The Charge of the Light Brigade", Tennyson is once again selecting and controlling the metre of his poem in order to fit with the nature and the feel of his subject matter.

Another metre poets have occasionally favoured is *trochaic* metre. This is, put simply, the inverse of iambic metre: a trochee is a two-syllable foot in which only the *first* syllable is stressed. Examples of single-word trochees in English are "**ne**ver", "**cert**ain", and "**pen**cil". This is a slightly less easy and natural metre for a poet to deploy, but there are examples of it in English language poetry – such as "Hiawatha" by the American poet Henry Wadsworth Longfellow:

> By the shore of Gitche Gumee,
> By the shining Big-Sea-Water,
> At the doorway of his wigwam,
> In the pleasant Summer morning,
> Hiawatha stood and waited.

The way the stress falls here at the beginning of each line – "**By** the **shore** of **Gitch**e **Gum**ee,/ **By** the **shin**ing **Big**-Sea-**Wat**er" – gives the poem a punchy, emphatic quality that is missing from iambic verse. A similar example of the effect of trochees can be found in William Blake's poem, "The Tyger", which begins as follows:

> Tyger Tyger burning bright
> In the forests of the night

Here, Blake is describing a ferocious beast designed, amongst other things, symbolically to represent all that is primal, frightening, and dynamic in nature. The particular kind of metre Blake uses here is called "catalectic" (or incomplete) trochaic tetrameter – the lines are made up of four trochees, but note how the final unstressed syllable is missing at the end of each one. This increases the punchy forcefulness of the lines even further, as they both begin <u>and</u> end with a stressed syllable. Once again, form reflects and helps to emphasise the content, as both these poets carefully and deliberately pick metrical patterns that suit their content and themes.

Conclusions: Free Verse and Metrical Meanings

Anyone reading this chapter would be forgiven for think-ing "hang *on* ... there are plenty of poems that simply *do not have* a regular metre. What about those? What am I sup-posed to do if I have to analyse one of them?" This would be an entirely fair and reasonable complaint – there are indeed many poems that have no regular metrical founda-tion. This is usually referred to as *free verse*, and has been particularly common and popular since the beginning of the twentieth century. Many poets over the last century or so have found the use of traditional, regular metre to be a rather limiting, constraining business. Instead, in an effort to innovate and break free into new literary terri-tory, they have chosen to produce work that is liberated from "metre" in any traditional sense. The American poet Robert Creeley complained that "form is never more than an extension of content": trying to write in regular metre, in other words, ends up meaning you have to distort what you really want to say by forcing it into an artificial formal structure. From this sort of perspective, it is better to dis-pense with regular metre altogether.

So: what are the best ways of approaching rhythm and metre if a poem is in "free verse", and lacks any regu-lar metre? There is no straightforward answer to this, but a good starting-point might be for us to go back to the example sentence of verse I used at the beginning of this

chapter. You will remember that one of the versions I used
ran as follows:

> Today I went out to the shops,
> And bought a loaf of bread.

In the light of our considerations of metre, it might now
be noticed that I was, in fact, sneakily organising the sentence here into two iambic lines: "Tod**ay** I **went** out **to**
the **shops**,/ And **bought** a **loaf** of **bread**". The regularity
of the lines gives a nice feeling of harmony and security to
the sentence. Let us compare it now with another of the
versions I used:

> Today I
>   went out
>
> to the shops
>   and bought
>   a
>   loaf of bread.

Here, of course, the very same words are being used. But
arranged like this – as free verse, with no regularity to
each line – the *feel* of the sentence is different. There is a
much greater sense of movement, of instability, with no
punctuation at the end of the lines (technically described
as *enjambment*), and the length and rhythm of each line
varying. This example gives some sense of the kinds of
effect free verse can create. It would be easy to make a
simple claim that regular metre suggests harmony, with

the irregularity of free verse suggesting disharmony –
but things are, of course, not quite so straightforward as
that. Free verse does not always connote disharmony, by
any means – but the varied patterns and rhythms of free
verse <u>do</u> open up a sense of dynamic change, of unpre-
dictability and unevenness and dissonance, that cannot
be captured within the constraints of a regular metrical
framework.

An excellent example of how free verse can be effectively used is "Praise Song for my Mother", by the Guyanese
poet Grace Nichols. This poem, in which the speaker
endeavours to highlight the various inspirational qualities of her mother, begins as follows:

> You were
> water to me
> deep and bold and fathoming

The link of the mother-figure to "water" provides her here
with essential, life-giving qualities. Throughout the poem,
very little punctuation is used, creating a primal, elemental
quality that helps to complement the depth and the vital-
ity of the bond between mother and child. In a poem of
celebration such as this one, the varying rhythms to each
line, and the varying line lengths, do not seem to create
disharmony so much as a feeling of simplicity and natu-
ralness. Though there is a background sadness, too – the
speaker addresses her mother in the past tense throughout
the poem ("You were [...] you were [...] you were"), implying that the mother has died – the overall tone is one of

joyous affirmation. The poem closes with the line "Go to your wide futures, she said": the mother has opened up all the many possibilities of life for her children, the sense of vast potential and opportunity emphasised here by the use of the plural "futures".

It is always helpful to think about form as, in some way, an expression of a poem's content – poets will choose a form that suits the subject matter, and the emotional substance, of the poem they wish to write. Sometimes this might actually involve a mixture of free verse and what we might call more "traditional" aspects of poetry, such as in "I Know Why the Caged Bird Sings" by Maya Angelou. In this poem, a contrast is generated between two birds – one caged, one free; it is not made explicit in the poem what these birds might represent, but Angelou was a significant civil rights activist in 1960s America, and readers have often interpreted the poem as a commentary on racial oppression, with the two birds metaphorically depicting the inequality between black and white citizens in American society. Some lines from the middle of this poem run as follows:

> The caged bird sings
> with a fearful trill
> of things unknown
> but longed for still
> and his tune is heard
> on the distant hill
> for the caged bird
> sings of freedom.

These very short lines are not quite regular; the metre changes in various ways from line to line. The heavy enjambment and absence of punctuation creates a sense of dynamic movement and instability, while the lack of harmony and regularity to the metre seems to fit with the emotional pain and trauma that the bird expresses and represents. The lines are held together, though, by the heavy use of rhyme; the brightness and musicality this brings to the lines sits uneasily with the more disrupted elements here, suggestive, perhaps, of the tension between the free expression that the bird yearns for, and its painful entrapment in the prison of its cage. In this poem, formal regularity and formal irregularity are tangled up with each other in subtle, moving, and effective ways.

All the examples in this chapter are designed to provide some suggestions regarding how to think about poetic form – for many students, the trickiest of all aspects of poetry. It can take some time to feel comfortable spotting what metre a poet might be utilising, what the significance of rhyme (or its absence) might be and what the overall shape of a poem and its organisation might reveal. The analysis of poetic form takes some practice. Most important of all is to avoid any oversimplified thinking about form: the reality is that there is never just "one answer" to what sorts of effects particular formal choices might convey. Aim to be as precise as possible – looking, say, at particular rhymes, or particular rhythms in certain lines that might be striking, or unusual, or out of place. Always consider the form of a poem <u>in connection with its content</u>. Do not forget that "feature spotting" is to be avoided at all costs. When we analyse form in poetry, we must always – as carefully as we can – make sure we focus on the *particular effects* that are created.

How to Write an Essay on a Poem

Essay Structure: A Five-Paragraph Model

There is no single correct way to structure an essay on a poem, and I do not want to suggest that there is. Different students, different teachers, might develop their own successful, individual strategies, and various different approaches to the construction of an essay can be equally effective. In addition, specific academic courses and examination syllabi often expect particular assessment criteria to be met: this can significantly affect how essays might need to be structured, in order to meet the mark schemes and examiners' requirements. The question of what the "right" essay technique might be, in other words, has different answers in different circumstances. Bearing all this in mind, what I want to put forward here is *one suggested way* in which an essay on a poem can be structured. It is basic, and it is simple. Most of all, it is *flexible* – the idea being that this structural framework might usefully be applied to various different kinds of English Literature assessment.

This is the point where everything we have looked at in previous chapters needs to come together into a fully realised, top-quality essay response. It is one thing to read a poem, and to pick out a number of analytical points you wish to make about it. The successful structuring of an essay response, though, is a different challenge. We might have numerous excellent points to make about a poem – but if we were simply to list these, one by one, our response would feel very confused, a chaotic blur of ideas. Like any piece of writing, a successful essay needs to be carefully organised. The model I want to propose is a clear five-paragraph structure involving an introduction, three main paragraphs, and a conclusion. The format works as follows:

Introduction

It is very easy to write a bad introduction, and not so easy to write a good one. There are a lot of very, *very* bad introductions out there. Many introductions simply re-state the question – or say something terribly vague like "In this poem, there are various interesting themes that I am going to explore". An introduction should *not* just be a brief, throwaway sentence or two: it is a serious mistake to think that, actually, the real analysis in an essay starts in the second paragraph. A good introduction should be two things: it should be **precise**, and it should be **sophisticated**. It needs to show, straight away, that you have a *complex* understanding of the poem you wish to discuss: that you have noticed ambiguities in the writing, for example, or that you have a sense of the poem's "surface" and "deep" meanings. It also needs a sense of precision – vagueness is always our enemy. Ideally, we need to find something to quote in our introduction. My suggestion here, in this model, is that the introduction is the perfect place to analyse a poem's *title*. This is a great way of giving some analytical sharpness to the introductory paragraph – and as indicated in Chapter 1, there is almost always something relevant and significant to say about a title.

Main Paragraph #1: Language & Imagery

There must be no misunderstanding here – it is extremely important to quote and analyse details in *every* paragraph of an essay. The last thing I want to suggest is that this paragraph is the only one in which you should analyse a poet's use of language. But it is a good idea to frame a paragraph specifically around the way language is used. Pick out a few key individual words, ideally, about which you feel particularly confident: the idea is to give a sharp and precise explanation of some of the language choices the poet has made. There might be some particular moments of description – or perhaps some similes or metaphors – that seem to you to be especially important, and on which you might comment.

Main Paragraph #2: Atmosphere, Mood & Tone

Essentially, this paragraph is designed to focus on the *emotional content* of the poem. What is the poem's mood? Is it a happy poem, or is it sad, angry, disappointed, regretful? There may well be more than one answer to this question – in fact, I would suggest that a good essay is always likely to pick out more than one emotional dimension to any poem. The atmosphere and mood may change at a particular point, or various points, as the poem progresses. Once again, it is important to convey a complex sense of the poem here in your discussion of its emotional content, delivering some precise analysis of details as you do so.

Main Paragraph #3: Form & Structure

This is the paragraph where all of our discussions in the previous chapter come into play. Consider all the various ways in which the poem might be shaped – its stanza structure, the rhythm and metre, the rhyme (if it has any), the overall sense of regularity or irregularity it presents. Remember that we must avoid "feature spotting" at all costs – it is crucial to think carefully about the precise *effect* that these various aspects of the form might have. Consider, too whether the overall structure of the poem – how it progresses from beginning to end – might involve any shift or turning points that might be usefully analysed.

Conclusion

Conclusions are much like introductions – it is very easy to write a bad one, but putting together a successful conclusion is a rather more difficult art. A conclusion needs to do rather more than just re-state what you have already said. Ideally, you need to tie the threads of your essay together into a sophisticated series of comments that encapsulate the various key ideas that the poem displays. Much like with your introduction, it is very useful to make some textual reference in your conclusion, in order to create a sense of precision. Try to "save" a final analytical point for this concluding paragraph: something that relates to the final line or two of the poem may be particularly useful here.

Example Essay and Commentary

I want to end this guide with an example of an essay. This is designed to demonstrate how the five-paragraph model I have just outlined might be utilised in practice. It is also intended to show how some of the analytical strategies I have been describing throughout the book might be incorporated into an essay response. Put simply, the best way of explaining how to write an essay on a poem is by direct demonstration of some good practice.

The poem I have chosen as the object of focus is a well-known sonnet by William Wordsworth. In order to keep things fairly simple, I will frame the essay around a fairly straightforward, accessible question. Alongside the essay, notes will be provided that explain exactly what I am doing in each paragraph, and why.

Question: Discuss the poet's presentation of the city in the following poem

Composed Upon Westminster Bridge, September 3, 1802

by William Wordsworth

Earth has not anything to show more fair:
Dull would he be of soul who could pass by
A sight so touching in its majesty:
This City now doth, like a garment, wear
The beauty of the morning; silent, bare,
Ships, towers, domes, theatres, and temples lie
Open unto the fields, and to the sky;
All bright and glittering in the smokeless air.
Never did sun more beautifully steep
In his first splendour, valley, rock, or hill;
Ne'er saw I, never felt, a calm so deep!
The river glideth at his own sweet will:
Dear God! the very houses seem asleep;
And all that mighty heart is lying still!

Essay Response

Introduction

In this poem, Wordsworth presents the city of London as a strikingly beautiful and powerful space. His emphasis is on conveying a sense of unity and harmony, both in terms of the city's component parts, and also in its relationship with the surrounding elements of the natural world.[1] Wordsworth's title references "Westminster Bridge" – a man-made structure within the city – and significantly, he focuses throughout the poem on the city's structures and buildings, rather than on the people who live within it. There is a personalised feel to the title through the specific reference to the date of composition, "September 3, 1802". This conveys the impression of a diary entry, and fits with the emphasis throughout the poem on the speaker's own personal, emotional response to the city scene as he looks upon it. The recording of the specific date in this manner also suggests a special level of significance to this particular moment.[2]

---

1   My first main aim in this introduction is to summarise the poem's key themes and ideas – that's what my first two sentences here are all about.

2   In order to give my introduction more precision, I then get my teeth into the title – this tends to work well, and Wordsworth's title here is ripe for analysis. Notice there are several distinct

Main Paragraph #1: Language & Imagery

One of the ways in which Wordsworth highlights the beauty of the city is through his use of language. The very first line – "Earth has not anything to show more fair" – immediately elevates the city above the terrestrial plane, giving it proximity to heaven and a sense of it possessing divine qualities.[3] There is an implication here, too, that nature – more frequently the subject of praise for its beauty, and more often Wordsworth's source of inspiration – is, in fact, no more beautiful that this urban scene.[4] Later in the poem, the sunrise is described as no more splendid when it shines on "valley, rock, or hill": in other words, this urban sunrise is just as beautiful as its rural counterpart. Much of the language emphasises a feeling of harmony. The city's

---

    points to make about it, not just one: this helps bring a sense of complexity to this introduction, as I unpick the title's various ambiguous meanings. The result is a nice, sharp, detailed paragraph – I've managed to avoid making the introduction feel throwaway here.

3   It is often pretty useful to start with a poem's first line, so that's what I do here, in order to explain the reader's first impressions of the speaker's feelings.

4   I allow myself one contextual point here: that Wordsworth is more often known for writing about nature, not cities (I have minimised any references that assume knowledge of the poet, or historical context – there are potential points to make, for instance, about the industrial revolution, but I have not included these in the essay).

buildings "lie/open unto the fields", the enjambment here highlighting the oneness of urban and rural spaces, the city merging with both "fields" and "sky". Personification is used in order to emphasise further this sense of optimistic unity. The river is personified as a free and autonomous being, moving at "his own sweet will", the word "sweet" implying pleasure and happiness. In an image suggestive of close physical contact, the city wears the morning's beauty as a "garment". The utopian atmosphere that surrounds this scene is encapsulated by Wordsworth's reference to the "smokeless" air. In this perfected urban setting, where the buildings are "bright" and glittering", there is no pollution, or grime, or factory smoke. At the same time, the background connotations of the word "smokeless" are somewhat darker: the word is a reminder that Wordsworth is presenting a particular snapshot of the city at the very beginning of the day, before it has come to life. The smokelessness of this moment is simultaneously a signal that the smoke and pollution of the city will inevitably emerge when the working day begins.[5]

5   It is always particularly useful if your language examples in this paragraph can relate to individual words, as this delivers an automatic precision to your analysis. That is what I do here with the focus on words such as "sweet" and (in particular) "smokeless". Regarding the latter, I am careful to unpick some *ambiguity* in the associations of this particular word, as it can be read in a couple of different ways.

Main Paragraph #2: Atmosphere, Mood & Tone

The overarching mood of this poem is one of strong optimism and positivity. The scene is described as "touching" in line 3, and much of the poem articulates the force and power of the speaker's emotional response.[6] Towards the end of the poem, the use of repeated exclamation marks indicates the intensity of the speaker's emotional state. In particular, the exclamation "Dear God!" exhibits astonishment and wonder at the beauty and tranquillity of the sleeping houses; it also resonates with the implications in the opening lines that the cityscape possesses a divine level of majesty. There is a kind of contrast in the poem between the deep tranquillity of this scene and the emotional intensity of the speaker's response to it, with the speaker exclaiming in response to the "calm" of the scene and the city's "still" heart. This discrepancy between scenic tranquillity and the speaker's internal passion is encapsulated in the poem's very final moments – with the final word, "still", indicating peacefulness but injected with emotional force by the exclamation mark that follows it.[7]

6   Once again, I am trying to sustain a good level of precision here by picking out and commenting upon an individual word from the poem.

7   In many ways, this is quite a tricky poem to analyse with regard to atmosphere and tone, as there seems really to be one answer – the poem is straightforwardly optimistic and positive. It raises the question of how we might be sophisticated or complex about

Main Paragraph #3: Form and Structure

Wordsworth's poem is a sonnet – a fourteen-line form
that is traditionally associated with order and harmony.
The formal intricacy of the sonnet is especially appropriate for Wordsworth's focus on the unified quality of the
cityscape he describes.[8] The intricate rhyme scheme mimics
the intricate, complementary interrelationship of the city's
buildings, as well as providing a brightness and music that
is consistent with the positivity of the overall description.[9]
The underlying use of iambic pentameter provides a harmonious rhythmic undercurrent to the poem, whilst also
making deviations from this template especially significant.
For instance, the twelfth line, describing the gentle flow
of the river, is quite regularly iambic in a manner that is
appropriate to the undulating flow of the water itself: "The
river glideth at his own sweet will". It is followed, though,
with a strong spondee in the next line, as the overwhelmed
speaker exclaims in response to the beauty and tranquillity

---

the emotions expressed in a poem when things seem, at that level,
to be quite one-dimensional. What I do here is to focus on a contradiction that is present: the scene is emphasised as very calm,
but the speaker himself is intensely emotional. This allows me to
create a multi-dimensional feel to my analysis in this paragraph.

8   I begin here with a fairly straightforward link between
     Wordsworth's choice of form and the subject matter of his poem.

9   In my comment on rhyme here, I manage to pick out two differ-
     ent ways of interpreting its effect in the poem.

of the scene: "<u>Dear</u> <u>God</u>!" The spondaic stress on both these monosyllables helps to convey the emotional force of the speaker's words.[10]

Conclusion

Wordsworth's poem is a passionate celebration of the London cityscape, and he treats it throughout like an object of beauty very much comparable in grandeur and magnificence to the beauteous forms of the natural world. This emotional positivity is very much the dominant component of the poem's atmosphere and mood: the only darker and bleaker shadows are only ever noticeable as a subtle undercurrent to the surface description, but they are there, especially in relation to the transience of the beauty by which the speaker is so moved. In the final line, for instance, the "mighty heart" of the personified city is "lying still" – a highly positive note on which to end the poem, indicating the city's power as well as its peacefulness. Once again, though, there is a contrasting undercurrent: the implication of the *sleeping* city is that this tranquillity

---

10 Here, my comments on metre focus on a moment of divergence from the poem's overall iambic base. There are several moments where Wordsworth gently distorts the iambic pentameter – the moment of exclamation here is a particularly useful one to pick out, as there is a clear link between the use of two stressed syllables and the emphatic emotion the speaker is conveying.

is a temporary state, and the city will soon wake into a much more turbulent, noisy, chaotic reality. Part of the preciousness of this scene is its fragility as a very specific moment that is destined to evaporate once the daily life of the city sparks into being.[11]

11   Much like with introductions, a conclusion can easily feel thin and throwaway. I combat this here by making sure that, in my final paragraph, I make some specific reference to the text – the final line of the poem is often a good place to go in conclusions, and this is precisely what I do here. The point I make is especially useful, as it complicates the overall sense of optimism in the poem – meaning that I end the essay with a sense of sophistication and complexity. My final few sentences here show that, even in a poem of apparently uncomplicated celebration, I am able to highlight a form of underlying ambiguity.

Glossary

Ambiguity: the existence of more than one meaning or avenue of interpretation (see pages 9–17).

Dactyl: a three-syllable foot (or unit) of rhythm following a stressed-unstressed-stressed pattern (see pages 48–49). *DUM - di - di*

Enjambment: the running on of sense from one line to the next without any punctuation at the line's end (see pages 52–55).

Form: a term, in poetry, to describe the various ways in which language is shaped or arranged (see pages 33–56).

Free verse: poetry that does not follow any clear or regular metrical pattern (see pages 51–56).

Iamb: a two-syllable foot (or unit) of rhythm following an unstressed-stressed pattern (see pages 41–48). *di - DUM*

Iambic pentameter: the most common metre in English poetry – ten-syllable lines made up of five iambs, with every second syllable stressed (see page 43).

Metre: a term used to described the measurement of rhythm in lines of poetry (see pages 41–43).

Prose: writing that, in contrast to verse, is not arranged in lines (see pages 34–35).

Rhyme: the chiming of the same or similar word sounds (see pages 36–41).

7272727272722272727272722272727272727272

Rhythm: the natural pattern of stressed and unstressed syllables in language, measured as metre (see pages 41–42).

Sonnet: an especially famous traditional form of poem, fourteen lines in length (see pages 25 and 68).

Trochee: a two-syllable foot (or unit) of rhythm following a stressed-unstressed pattern (see pages 49–50).   DUM - di

Verse: words written out in lines, and therefore as poetry, with attention to the arrangement of these words and in relation to each other (see pages 34–35).

Bibliography

Further Reading

Brownjohn, Sandy, *The Poet's Craft: a Handbook of Rhyme, Metre and Verse* (London: Hodder & Stoughton, 2002).

Empson, William, *Seven Types of Ambiguity* (New York: New Directions, 1930).

Fry, Stephen, *The Ode Less Travelled: Unlocking the Poet Within* (London: Arrow, 2007).

Lennard, John, *The Poetry Handbook* (Oxford: Oxford University Press, 1996).

Padel, Ruth, *52 Ways of Looking at a Poem* (London: Vintage, 2004).

Parini, Jay, *Why Poetry Matters* (New Haven, CT: Yale University Press, 2008).

Stevenson, Anne, *About Poems: and how poems are not about* (Hexham: Bloodaxe, 2017).

Williams, Rhian, *The Poetry Toolkit: the Essential Guide to Studying Poetry* (London: Bloomsbury, 2013).

Online Sources Cited

Onwuemezi, Natasha, "Poetry Sales Are Booming, LBF Hears",
    13 April 2018, <https://www.thebookseller.com/news/
    poetry-summit-766826>.
Thompson, Nathan A., "Poetry slams do nothing to help the art
    form survive", 1 February 2013, <https://www.independent.
    co.uk/arts-entertainment/art/features/poetry-slams-do-noth-
    ing-to-help-the-art-form-survive-8475599.html>.

Index

9 781788 747288